Exploring the Intersection of Fame and Fortune

Exploring the Intersection of Fame and Fortune

Aria Nightingale

Contents

1

Introduction to the Study of Fame and Fortune in t

This book is about fame and fortune as they play out in the real lives of legendary celebrities and on their posthumous reputations. Among the legendary celebrities I take up, there are athletes, media personalities, and cultural figures like politicians—but most of them are stage and screen entertainers. They have had roles of various sizes, but all were of crucial importance in creating their legends. The focus on legendary celebrities sheds light on the ultimate evaluation criteria by which celebrities live or die. Unlike contemporary fame that is won through media blasts, we are more impressed by the legendary stars of yesterday than by today's celebrities who are with us here today and gone tomorrow. Once a promising tough guy at the box office, Marlon has thus become an irreplaceable cultural figure who signifies a certain 1950s style in an age when style itself is legendary.

The underlying question of why we become interested in the lives of celebrities is the last thing to tackle because interest in this question is first and foremost. This book will also bring out the classic dimension of entire fields of study in which fame and fortune are for the first time viewed via the lives of their outstanding participants. Becoming able celebrities is the product of effort over time, it does not generally refer to the entire time of the career of the celebrities taken up here. At the earliest, these reigning celebrities must leave behind them callow pursuits during which they strove to build their very first adult acts. Outside of such rare cases, the very construction of "the act" that ultimately makes them irreplaceable often occurs in the context of one or more published confessional accounts of their lives.

2

The Historical Evolution of Celebrity Culture

Celebrity culture and the desire for fame have evolved and changed as a phenomenon through history and modernity. Both the concept and its fulfillment have undergone different schemas and realities. Maybe this was not so evident in antiquity. In religious terms, every culture had its deities that armies were willing to die for. Nowadays, gods and goddesses are famous people from the past and present world, who live or lived high from a platform in the stratosphere where only gods and demigods used to hang out.

Celebrity was conceived for years. Historically, fame was something that did not last beyond the life of the individual. So there was no desire to acquire it, that is, there was no desire for that fame, but on the contrary, rejection of fame. On the contrary, they were frightened by the idea of infamy, which would last for generations, and had many measures to avoid it. Sentiments like those of the first lyric poets would be raised later by the tragic poets, who, on the occasion of exalting some ideal, also stigmatize the vanity of the human being, who, subject to the fatality of law, could not transcend as an individual. Medieval celebrity was embraced by the figure of the nobleman as something destined, since there was no possibility of individual ascension, but rather that of family. After years, the family evolved from the ancestral name to the surname, for the bourgeois and later democratic world.

3

The Psychology of Fame and Fortune: Understanding

Studies have shown that the richest actors are not necessarily the happiest. Many of us would choose fame and fortune over obscurity and oppression at any opportunity. However, what are the implications of becoming famous? In recent years, academic psychologists have turned their attention to something that was previously, in essence, reserved for the celebrity magazines. Indeed, the desires of many people make news. The psychology of fame and fortune is a reality today, addressing the various reasons why people want to be admired, the consequences and implications of celebrity life, and indeed the psychology governing the (often idiotic and impulsive) operation of celebrities.

The reason for contemplating our strange and cultural enthusiasm for fortune is often explained by studying the cultural world. This is a progression, as some areas of psychology must necessarily function by investigating self-selected samples of people who have accepted the cultural, and essentially arbitrary, enthusiasm that obviates the best part of the planet. The psychological studies that specify the psychological position of the famous have focused on the interview sample and explored the individual 'aftereffects' concerning other celebrities. Many perceive that famous people are well cared for, tough if they are paid to do so. While we invest resources in celebrities, we often mock them and question their relevance. Celebrity defects are one of the few gaffes that we agree are more likely to see in some celebrities.

4

Case Studies of Legendary Celebrities: Their Rise

Success in sport opens many doors. Players earn from their clubs through income, endorsements, advertising, and in some cases, ownership. As an elite athlete, David Beckham drew a large audience of fans, especially because of his durability in his peak. Beckham is a freekick specialist, and soccer commentators have stated the iconic nature of his freekick technique. As a social phenomenon, a technique of play becomes iconic through its association with an exceptional human being, or football player in the present moments. Beckham's career precluded the initiation of a more general range of studies of conversion of financial talent those are outsized returns. Beckham's management approach is high quality in addition to the optimal dose of formal training; a conscious overnight decision for his 1996 marriage enables optimal participation at the end of the relationship based on labor union economics.

Despite being the top 5% of the world's income earners, Beckham's net worth is not far from what we see in our social contacts these days. This shows that Beckham's on the field service activities, unlike his business franchising, are huge on the size of the world, but certainly not Peacock luxuriously above those who can call himself the top percentile. There was no essential change in his marketability in the opinions of talent agents in the United States, Britain, America, Cannes and Germany after being caught and admitted to the romp with the pretty girl chased by the police. "He had already open doors that everyone deserves it," said sports director for the football player. In my opinion, Beckhams of the sporting world try to stand out from those who are famous, who keep a friend paid salary by doing anything in particular, or paint the last Tito Wa. Peacock parade. Another Sports Manager summed up the attitude toward soccer and world famous clientele "Sometimes people made mistakes and that's life. David is strong personality and driven person. It is quite typical of the firm to maintain." The credibility of Beckham was clearly in the accumulation or the same, according to the managers of the celebrities.

Hollywood Icons: From Marilyn Monroe to Audrey Hepburn

Coinciding with these same years, Hollywood was creating its own pantheon of legends—Marilyn Monroe, Humphrey Bogart, Elizabeth Taylor, Tony Curtis and Sir Laurence Olivier, Paul Newman, Joanne Woodward, James Dean, and a Belgian actress named Audrey Hepburn, who, in 14 years with only 21 starring pictures, rose to the top of the Hollywood ladder of wealth and admiration, behind only Lillian Gish, in her lifetime, in a humanness that made her richer than her 10 movies, her one Academy Award, and her $2,120,538 fortune. If there was ever a movie star whose life seemed like a fairy tale, it was young Audrey Hepburn. The daughter of the Baron van Heemstra, former Dutch minister to France, she surfaced out of Belgium just after World War II, speaking several languages fluently but with uncertainty about which to choose, with the sort of background and assets to underscore the role of Gigi and to avoid wallowing in mud while she was making her first movie. The picture was little more than another cable of plot details, except for one scene in which Audrey comes into a small street—looks frightened at first—then sees a shop—looks fascinated—moves inside—spots a prince during a brief appearance—spends a tiring day getting somebody to buy her a hat, so she becomes like him—a tomboy in overalls with a turned-up lip—and finally prances off into the sunset as Frederique, the young ambassador's daughter. Audrey Hepburn came a free-lance gamin and a real actress in that one take. The shop was at 5 North Broadway, St. Louis, and, behind hundreds of potential stars, Audrey was in and gone in a day. But an Oberst's wife out on Government Hill was so impressed she notified a producer her husband had served with in persuasion of Audrey's potential, and later Lieutenant Colonel Coen promptly did the same. In New York, Broadway saw a great European dancer. The Ritz saw a young amateur who found all this very exciting. And Vasar saw a beautiful ingenue in 1951 to put in "Gigi"—spelled with only two i's—in Water Market. Starting November 24th at the La Ronde theater. Next stop Hollywood. As the ingenue, Audrey was to play the opposite of the hero—Joseph Cotten—on Kathryn Hays.

Music Legends: The Beatles, Michael Jackson, and Madonna

The Beatles. The term "favorite band" has become a bit of a cliché in modern vernacular. And yet, despite the wealth of music being produced today, the distinction of "favorite band" still isn't an uncommon way for the contemporaneously inclined to ask about musical preference. Whether one considers the cultural and musical impact in charting out a distinguished list or if the question is answered with shuffling feet and a dimly lit gaze, success has a visual sociological component. Elvis was a celebrity and, to an extent, a product of his time. And, once again in 2019 nostalgia, we remember him as a standalone figure who represented quite a bit; we also remember The Beatles.

Michael Jackson. Both sets of musicians were influenced by The Beatles, but he explored quite a few musical genres, including Motown, R&B, Soul, Funk, and contemporary Pop. He, like McCartney and Starr, maintained a visual aspect of success; Jackson wrote his own music, had his albums published, produced, and marketed, and managed to change the music landscape with Thriller - where people bought and listened to the album because of who he was. As a cultural icon, Michael Jackson evolved from a one-hit wonder to a renowned celebrity, one of how many? Charlie offers the following statistics: "Jackson has gained a world fame that only a handful of people share" and "Thriller's worldwide record sales were 45 million." Perhaps the most iconic band from the United States: The Beach Boys. As Alexander points out, these four musicians - The Beatles and The Beach Boys - were the "most widely acknowledged bands" of the 1960s.

Sports Superstars: From Muhammad Ali to Michael Jordan

One of the most well-known and beloved sportsmen in history, Muhammad Ali, was renowned around the globe and respected by fellow sportsmen, various nationalities, and individuals of all backgrounds. A well-known and affluent sportsman, Ali achieved fortune and fame in the boxing universe for his exciting and stringent battles, against numerous venerable rivals and through colorful and outspoken commercials. Throughout his career, Ali remained ahead of the athletic globe. "The Greatest" proclaimed himself, and his fantastic athletic ability was only matched by his biting wit, humor, audacity, and celebrity. Despite his eccentricity, he was admired and appreciated by many. He was recognized for his notoriety in the press, his friendship, and his talk-show appearances.

In his day, Jordan, known for his clothing, video advertisements, and billboards, was hailed as a major sports and marketing phenomenon. Marketing-seekers hurried to place his face on their products and video clippings. Air Jordan shoes, manufactured by Nike, were a commercial breakthrough. Jordan's footwear made him famous, and he has long been the greatest varsity basketball player. He retired from competitive basketball for the second time in 1999, at age 40. In his later career, he was the contemporary manager of the artists and D.C. Wizards president of basketball activities. Nike's "Air Jordan" collection, which debuted in the 1980s, remains highly popular, is a big commercial achievement, and brings millions in profit down the line for Nike and Jordan entrepreneurs. Even two decades later, Jordan's name can be seen in the shoe line. Nike was the protagonist of an overturned legal row in 2015. The company was issued a petition to stop the selling or marketing of any other items linking to the basketball star via Nike. Jordan is the marketing director for Nike and earns continuing benefits from the series. Jordan is also an entrepreneur and has a Corvette-dedicated dealership. In the 1990s and afterwards, a large number of star entertainers invested in the NBA. They have spread through the arena of National basketball, having tried broadcasting, notably as an expert on Phil Jackson's Chicago Bulls CONTENDER. With the Charlotte Bobcats, and the corresponding thing continues.

5

The Impact of Fame and Fortune on Personal Relatio

Operating well above the financial limit of the world, breaking records on film and television, and turning heads as soon as they appear in public – this is the life of the ultra-rich celebrity. As explored by the elite level of TMZ and celebrity gossip, being A-list famous and wealthy seems to be intertwined partners, and many of the biggest names often have massive paychecks. With the privilege and glamour of becoming a recognizable figure also comes the effervescent nature of the lifestyle that it entails. Starring long Hollywood veterans and die-hard stars alike, here is the life of the rich and famous, struggling with interpersonal relationships at the same time.

Jennifer Lawrence, during interviews and lengthy feature pieces in magazine profiles, has spoken often about her relationship with her Victoria and Abdul director, Darren Aronofsky. As their love blossomed from the set of their film, such passion also led to an unfortunate separation at the conclusion of their passion-driven union. Every week, perhaps because of the intimacy she instilled as a result of birthing director Aronofsky's visual children, their love crumbled faster than it began. This is often the outcome of many Hollywood divorces and relationship woes, playing their lives with history. The proverb "you don't know what you have until it's gone" even applies to our greatest celebs, including Jennifer Aniston and Brad Pitt. Mixing business with pleasure and involving your partner in your work happens to be a sin of the union. The identity you have created for yourself on HBO isn't the person they beg the pleasure to get to know when it comes to your personal life.

6

Celebrity Philanthropy: The Intersection of Wealth

Intertwining wealth and philanthropy, celebrity or superstar philanthropy has proven to be a unique and multifaceted instrument. Charitable contributions may vary from smaller, individual expressions of compassion or concern for others to financial donations of substantial magnitude to causes and organizations. For various reasons, celebrities can withdraw from their bank accounts for charitable purposes. They might do so to raise public awareness for a particular charity, to curb negative press, or for the effects of their financial contributions. The intersection in celebrity studies is filled with ethical, moral, economic, and feminist implications, and for further information, one should consider celebrity endorsements, commercial advertising, and celebrity representation in media.

In recent years, stars have been donating ever-increasing sums of money to a variety of social and humanitarian causes. Celebrities have been applauded, in the media, by the public and amid several ways of cultural organization for their significant financial contributions to charity work and philanthropy. Highlighted as compassionate and generous, many celebrities are praised for giving back in one way or another. As fans and supporters of charity, popular figures have become the true philanthropic champions of the 21st century. Camelot may have its knights and valiant leaders, but if modern-day knighthood exists at all, it exists in the hands of those in the public limelight. Most of the initial celebs-with-conscience coverage had more to do with the amount of money given by celebrities to their designated charities. It has also generally been reported that celebrities make more money when they execute a large, selfless donation.

7

The Dark Side of Fame and Fortune: Scandals, Addic

Despite living seemingly glamorous lives with money to spare and legions of fans vying for their attention, not everything always comes up roses for our favorite show-biz kings and queens. Scandals, arrests, addictions, and mental health issues can sometimes lurk right around the corner of a celeb's life. In these situations, it becomes increasingly difficult to know exactly how to handle a sensitive subject such as famous and mental health because the celebrity's privacy has to be protected in accordance with the law, but also because of the emotional toll it can take on those buying their albums or watching them on the big screen. It's easy to pay attention to the news reports, so let's take a closer look at exactly what happens when fame and mental health clash in the real world.

While it's true that Hollywood fun in the sun is a scene with staying power, Tinseltown and fame have become just as well-known for taking these bleary ODs first. Everyone from actors to rock stars to models has likely at least dabbled in drugs, either for the high or for medicating pain from arthritis. Everything from weed to prescription medication to the dreaded crack and hallucinogens has ever hit the sticky floor. Some sensitive celebrities, unable to bear the weight of their own lives, have gone their own ways permanently, either by taking too many meds or taking too sharp a razor to their wrists. Scandals and addiction are no strangers to fame and fortune around here. Assuming it is still wanted, one's mental health can be an entirely different game. Some classic celebrity stories really break our hearts and make us rethink the whole headline worth it. Where addiction is sometimes an external factor, mental health battles are particularly difficult because you carry the battlefield with you everywhere you go, and the ringmaster, of course, is the celebrity themselves.

8

The Role of the Media in Constructing Celebrity Na

The construction, maintenance, and zag of these celebrity narratives are the work of a powerful panoptic engine: the media. Media organizations choose which stories to cover based on their potential to attract an audience, a process often referred to as "news values" or "journalistic gatekeeping." Many celebrities and fans have long recognized that a day's news agenda is the product of a negotiation between celebrity representatives and the news media. The ultimate objective of this negotiation is to answer the Rubicon-curve question: What do people talk about around the water cooler? Hard news stories such as the war in Iraq and the genocide flooding in Darfur, or soft news stories about Paris Hilton's brief stay at a California detention center and the Josephson family sextuplets?

Astute public relations practitioners like Howard Rubenstein understand that media security is core to the negotiation process. They invest a great deal of effort in managing the news by negotiating what stars and star wrestlers call "soft news" front-stage stories (uplifting myths of redemption) and "backstage stories" (hard news that transcends fans' dry-text literacy), as David Maraniss and Daniel Boorstin, respectively, described them. Nir Rosen, a journalist for

Rolling Stone, said in an interview about the rise of celebrity television news that "the qualities that make a journalist into a celebrity are the very qualities that disqualify him or her from being a journalist - ego, vanity, narcissism... I credit myself with one scoop, and I know of many journalists who take credit for headlines they did not write, or stories they did not report. The danger here is that reporters start to believe that, just like they can create a story, they can bring celebrities down." Celebrity journalists have been accused of going soft on their famous news sources by practicing "infotainment" or what Leibovitz calls "new-dogism." The rapid growth of paparazzi who hound celebrities and other famous people to obtain sexual, illegal, or unethical photographs (often naked images) also illustrates the fine line between permissible and positive press behavior.

9

Fame and Fortune in the Digital Age: Social Media

Before there were walkathons, there were tent-armistice. This project seeks to support the creation and publication of worlds through the unusual characters of real people. While traditional and vintage celebrity life has its fair share of attention whores, some are so subtle as to be secretive, belonging with family to sane housewives riveted by the American obsession with fame. On the other hand, it marks the spark of stardom in the spark of a star.

Anyone with a phone and a dream can now broadcast themselves to an audience. This section suggests that it would be fruitful to explore the intersection of fame and fortune against this backdrop of the digital fame industry. The idea that the very product that influencers are selling is their own personality and personal life suggests the unique challenges of engaging in this professional venture. Given the ongoing work being done on the pursuit of celebrity and fame in the digital age, this project would also examine the evolution of the concept, noting distinctions between early thoughts on the subject and the intersection with traditional celebrity aspiration.

10

Gender and Diversity in Celebrity Culture

Gender and diversity in celebrity culture. Shifting gender dynamics have made celebrity and fame an increasingly enjoyable prerogative of both men and women. Together, for example, Jolie and Pitt function as the postmodern culmination of all our sexual idealizations and offer the promise of our own sexual prowess through participation in their playing field of travel. These stars give evidence of how the consumption of fame may serve as the validation of one's own tastes, not only through the purchase of fashion products, but also by the acquisition of the very people who are taste arbiters.

While there exist several discrete commentaries on fame and diversity discussed in the literature review, what has been missed thus far, however, is the validation of a life spent in the search for a personal pot of gold at the end of the rainbow, regardless of the contributor's marginalized diversity. Quite accidentally, the study of celebrity is on the vanguard of exploring this new world, in part, just because innovative, diverse exemplars of fame such as Ru Paul, Angelina Jolie, Johnny Depp, and Ricky Martin broke in. All celebrities such as these examples "can help to underline the humanizing function of the close-up – to suggest that the famous may indeed be 'just like us'. Despite the weight of cultural heritage that we bring to close-ups of those who seem most different from us, these close-ups may also enlarge our notion of who counts as gloriously, uniquely, human."

11

The Business of Celebrity: Endorsements, Branding,

In the context of today's omnipresent knowledge regarding the lifestyles, loves, and locales of the rich and famous known simply as "celebrity," it is easy to forget the ways in which commercially savvy front office owners and image professionals endeavor to craft, control, or cultivate the public personas of celebrities who stand in as the public faces of their institutions, corporations, trusts, wares, or other business entities. While the GVP above—the traded baseball player swathed in the wisdom of Neptune—probably is not expecting to share commercial endorsements with the billionaire owners imparting dead presidents bearing his approximate likeness to other baseball players willing to throw balls and hit sticks for a living, aligning oneself with well-known brands as a recognizable figure is something at which some of the new celebrity owners, our current baseball player celebrities, are increasingly adept.

The purpose of this business section of the anthology is to elucidate the commercial aspects of celebrity; many of the legends we treat doubled as yesterday's famous and the famous of today, and this section is concerned with providing more details regarding the kinds of strategies that prompted Sports Illustrated to announce in

2014 that some of the best tippers are "celebrities, especially athletes." Some of the stars we have written or read about in this anthology, very far from going unrecognized in their own time, derived lifestyles arising from their real lives even as the world knew them to be larger than life.

12

Legal and Ethical Issues in Celebrity Management

Handling the career of a celebrity involves making different sorts of agreements. In this chapter, we will analyze the legal issues related to contracts and image rights. Every professional handling a celebrity should be aware of the different regulations that can apply in a specific territory, as these can differ greatly from one jurisdiction to another. Also, while certain agreements are common in the management business, the precise terms can be adapted to suit particular clients' situations. In addition, professionals should be aware of the legal and ethical issues that can emerge in this sector and need to consider these aspects when advising and handling their clients.

Some agreements are specific to the areas in which image rights are exploited. Some potential deals can be made, others not. Further issues of images can arise through the possibility of defamation or passing off. Legal action can be taken if a photographer claims to be an authorized one to sell image material. Legal judgments might not be enough on their own, and a strategy has to be put into place to inform the general public that a certain person has not agreed to a particular agreement. Finally, even public archives can fail to obtain the appropriate clearances. An exception can be represented by historical images, genuinely in the public domain. Ethically speaking, images of misdeeds can be annoying to a famous person, even after the event. This is even more likely if the victim is a child. Some agents take legal action in this direction.

13

The Future of Fame and Fortune: Trends and Predict

What challenges and opportunities does the future hold for the "fame and fortune" of celebrities? The structure and workings of the intersection of fame and fortune have changed little over the past several decades, as evidenced in the thousands of magazine covers we surveyed from the 2000s and early 2010s. But the future might well be different. Indications are that celebrities are being propelled to wealth and fame in slightly different ways than in the past, and once they get there, we know less about their financial lives than at almost any other time. As such, we see three potential ways in which the future might differ from the past: changes in talent development and public stature, income generation once already in the public eye, and wealth distribution.

Our small bit of celebrity forecasting is, on balance, rosy. If the nature of the "celebrity industrial complex" is changing, it is imperative that we understand how the lives of celebrities are transforming along with, or in response to, these changes. However, with all of the benefits, celebrity can have a dark side: in short, controversy sells. In today's fast-paced world, overshadowed by high-profile scandals and tragedies, the methods by which celebrities become famous and wealthy may change. But the sensational overshadows the banal. In general, we are quite bad at forecasting the future. However, it is our sincere hope that by shedding some light on the advances and challenges in the "future of fame," we can spark important conversations that help make the path to fame and fortune a bit more navigable.

14

Conclusion: Insights and Reflections on the Real L

This report began with a proposition: that inquiry and contemplation are both appropriate means with which to examine the meaning of fame and fortune in the real lives of the celebrities who have devoted their energies to their accumulation. As some of the most extraordinary worldly privileges known to modern society, what this collection has sought to do is take small steps down a variety of pathways amongst the immensity of data that was shared with us by the 75 personalities who responded to the Ain't I Something survey. The exercise was not meant to hand down truths from Olympus; rather, the aim was to weave together a selection of what was uncovered, thereby enabling our participants to speak across the chapters for the reader to encounter and reflect upon what was said. From songwriting to entrepreneurship and business acumen, estate planning to digital rights and earnings, internal and external factors, professional advising to instinctive responses – all manner of issues in the interplay between these two axes have found a place in these pages.

The same goes for the many different and often complex relationships at play within elite entertainers as they go about pursuing these advantages, benefits, and more generally, desirable states and qualities. Considered from moment to moment, the described lived experiences of our survey respondents are indeed complex, ambiguous, and so profoundly specific. It is for this reason that many of the public-facing will always encourage thoughts to be carried deeper once more. Execution neither bars nor absolves; it web-plays. The simple fact of the matter is that for either or both fame and fortune to appear in such an ideal light, to appear as a gloriously streamed unison, the narrow sweet spot is present. Knowing more about how and when it was ever thought otherwise, and following this revelation to its least-thought terminus, would surely be a worthwhile expedition. And so we close our explorations, knowing further explorations yet await. As ever, the pages of the "whence and whither" are ours to speculate and spin.